EFFECTIVE WAYS TO BOOST SELF-ESTEEM

Chapter 1: Be optimistic for a happier life

A positive outlook for a positive life

Our attitude towards life in general plays a big part in how happy and successful we are in life. A person who is calm, calm, and always smiling, rather than someone who is stressed out and frowns.

The way you think and feel affects not only you but also those around you. In short, our mood affects our day. Developing and maintaining a positive attitude is essential if you want to live a positive and fulfilling life.

There are many ways to develop a more positive attitude and start changing the way you think and feel about the many situations you encounter in your daily life. It takes time to change your attitude and not return to negative thoughts, but eventually the new attitude becomes second nature. Here are the 5 most important points to remember when changing your attitude.

1. Change your mind-set to positive thinking and practice positive thinking every day. Focus on doing one task at a time and only think about the positive outcome and how you feel when you complete the task. Never give up doubt, let yourself think you've gone too far and just keep going. 2. Don't be negative in the conversation when it's easy for others to let you down. Especially if you have a negative outlook on life. Don't fall back into old patterns, turn negative stories into positive ones, and look for the good in every situation.

3. Look for good things in your environment and point them out. In this way, you can promote a positive attitude to those around you. 4. Always look for the good in whatever you do in your daily life. It might be a boring job that you don't normally like, it might feel negative, but try to find something. It turns into a more positive situation.

5. Don't let distractions or the temptation to go back to negativity. It takes time to change the way you feel and think. When you've been depressed about yourself and the world for too long, it takes time for your new settings to take effect. Stay logged in.

Over time, you will realize that you can change many areas of your life simply by changing your attitude from negative to more positive. You may find that your self-esteem improves, you become more popular, you become happier and more confident than before, you are able to tackle tasks you once hated without causing stress or anxiety, and your relationships improve. These are just some of the areas where you can improve yourself, develop a more positive attitude, and live a more positive life. Knowing your worth has nothing to do with checking your bank balance. We give others respect, love and compassion, but how often do we give ourselves what we deserve? How we value ourselves depends on our self-esteem. Self-esteem shows how much you value yourself. Healthy self-esteem leads to independence, well-being, and flexibility, the ability to adapt easily to change, cooperation, and a positive attitude in any situation. Poor health or low self-esteem, on the other hand, only leads to irrational thoughts, unhappiness, fear of the new, rigidity, defensiveness, and a negative outlook on life in general.

How we see ourselves has a lot to do with how others see us. When we are happy, smiling, and confident, others see us as people they want to be with. If we respect ourselves and show others respect you too, after all, how can we expect respect from others if we don't respect ourselves? So finding and cultivating self-esteem is cultivating self-esteem. Let's take a look at self-esteem.

High self-esteem

If you have a high self-esteem you will see certain traits in yourself and how you see yourself, traits linked with a high self-esteem or self-worth are

- You are secure about who you are and have confidence in your abilities
- You allow yourself to show your true feelings to others
- You don't have intimacy problems in relationships
- You are able to recognize and take pride in yourself for your achievements in life
- You are easily able to forgive yourself for mistakes and also forgive others

Low self-esteem

Similarly if you have problems with self-worth or low self-esteem then you will follow a certain pattern in your thoughts and ways, if you have problems with low self-esteem then you will see the following points in yourself

• You lack belief in yourself and are very insecure

• You have problems showing and accepting intimacy in relationships

• You never let your true feelings show

• You never recognize and give yourself credit for your accomplishments

• You have the inability to forgive yourself or others

• You resist change at every opportunity

Developing your self-worth

There are plenty of ways in which you can boost your self-esteem and change to a more positive and healthy outlook about yourself, here are some tips for developing and boosting your self-worth.

• Don't take other people's criticism to heart, instead listen to what they are saying and learn from it.

• Take some time out for yourself every day, meditate, look inside yourself and realize all your good points and imagine changing your bad ones into more positive.

• Celebrate and pride yourself on even the smallest achievements that you accomplish.

• Do something every day that you enjoy, such as talking a walk in the sunshine or soaking in a bubble bath.

• Never give up on something you enjoy doing, even if you know you shouldn't.

• Talk positively to yourself and repeat affirmations to expel negative thoughts and feelings.

Benefits of positive self-talk

One of the greatest influences we can use in life to our advantage is ourselves. Especially since we have access to thoughts that influence our emotions, they have a huge impact on how we approach life in general. You can give yourself more control over all aspects of your life by learning to control your self-talk and turning it into positive self-talk instead of the negative self-talk that most people unconsciously do throughout their day.

Your ability to succeed in life is highly dependent on how you approach life. A positive mental attitude leads to a more confident and ultimately more successful person than a negative one that leads to lack of self-confidence and low self-esteem. By taking a positive attitude you look at life in a different way to one of negativity, a positive attitude leads to seeing good in people and the world which leads to optimism and success. Your quality of life is based on how you think and feel from moment to moment and changing the way you think can drastically change how you see life and deal with life.

The person who goes through life optimistically with a positive attitude is better able to deal with life and the problems which it sometimes throws at us, they are able to bounce back and recover from problems or set-backs in life. The optimistic person will see the problem for what it is, nothing but a temporary set-back which they can overcome and move on, when looking at life in this optimistic way the person is able to take full control over their thoughts and feelings and turn a negative situation into a more positive one by simply altering the way they think. Since thoughts can either be positive or negative and you can only have one thought in mind at any one time then choosing positive will keep your thoughts, feelings and actions optimistic which leads to a happier person who is able to achieve their goals much easier.

Using positive self-talk in your daily life

You should use positive self-talk throughout the day in order to establish a new thinking pattern, you will probably have established a pattern of negative thinking for many years and this will take time to overcome, to start with you should aim to repeat positive self-talk around 50 times throughout the day, this can be achieved by repeating positive statements quietly to yourself or out aloud. Positive self-talk can be used for many different aspects in your life, it can help you to overcome difficult situations, gain more confidence in yourself, help you to quit habits, recover quicker from illness or make changes to your life in general. Popular phrases or sentences that can be used in positive self-talk include:

• I have an interesting challenge facing me – this could be used when a problem occurs in life or there is some difficulty, rather than looking at the situation in a negative way and thinking I have a problem, thinking of it as a challenge is a much more positive way of dealing with it.

• I like the person I am – this could be used to bolster self-confidence and gain respect about yourself and the person you are, similar statements could be “I am the best”, “I am a good person” or “I have many excellent qualities”.

• I know I can do this – This can be used when faced with a specific task that you never thought you could do before. Similarly, you can say "I have the ability to do this" or "It doesn't matter". It's a problem for me."

• I Am Full of Health, Energy and Vitality – This can be used to promote a good mood about your health, whether you are recovering from illness or post-illness.

• I am happy as a person - This can be used to encourage generally positive thinking about yourself and the world in which you live.

How Positive Affirmations Can Change Your Life

A positive attitude is the key to living a happy and successful life. Our thoughts play a big role in how we feel and while positive thinking leads to a happy and confident person in life, negativity leads to low self-esteem and many things in life. We unconsciously talk about how to get out of things many times, and every day hundreds of negative thoughts flow freely into our minds, letting ourselves get too low and becoming a seed of doubt. To change these negative thoughts and instil more positive thoughts, there are simple tools you can use throughout your day. Using daily positive affirmations can dramatically change your life for the better. You can change your life for the better in terms of

What is a positive affirmation? Positive affirmations can be used anywhere and anytime throughout the day. The more you use it, the easier it is for positive thoughts to replace negative thoughts, and you will begin to see benefits in your life. Affirmations are simple techniques to change the negative self-talk that we are mostly unaware of to view our lives in a more positive way. Most of us have been plagued with negative thoughts for years, so you can't change your thoughts and mind-set overnight, but if you stick with your affirmations, retraining your mind-set will pay off. There are many different affirmation techniques for dealing with different situations, and the most popular and successful ones are listed below.

Mirror technique

This technique helps you take care of yourself and develop confidence and self-esteem. Stand in front of a mirror, preferably full body, in your underwear or preferably naked. Start at the head and work your way down the body. Say out loud what you like about your body. For example, you can say, "I like the shine of my hair, the slight difference in colour where the light hits it" or "My eyes are a beautiful shade of. Glitter and shine. My eyes are a great feature. ”Take time to slowly examine your whole body and build a more positive image of yourself.

Technique everywhere

This technique can be used anytime, anywhere. Whenever you find yourself thinking negative thoughts, remember to mentally turn the volume knob down. Then think of a positive affirmation to replace the negative and repeat it to yourself to restore the volume.

Trash can technique

If you have negative thoughts, write them down on a piece of paper, roll the paper into a ball, and throw it in the trash. I'm here.

Meditation techniques

Find a quiet place to relax for five to ten minutes, close your eyes, and free your mind from all thoughts and emotions. Concentrate on the words you're repeating and start affirming yourself over and over again while believing what you're saying.

Chapter 2: It's all in our heads

Focus positively

We all go through difficult times in life. That's life. It's not always a bed of roses. But life is what you make it, and being positive in both the bad and the good times can make all the difference and get you through the tough times with a smile on your face.

But the big question is, "How can I stay positive when things get tough?" Staying optimistic during times like these should be the last thing on your mind, but the first thing you need to think more positively than ever before. The key to staying positive is to forget your problems and worries and recharge your batteries. This is especially true when you're having a bad day and you feel sorry for yourself and want to sit and cry. Here are some tips. • If there are people around you who have a negative attitude, stay away from them. Negativity spreads from person to person and it drags you along.

• Don't sit in front of the TV for hours. The news is depressing, police stations show violence and deaths, and almost every show has some form of negativity. If you watch TV, choose more positive programs. B. A nature documentary or comedy that shows the wonderful world in all its glory.

• Aim to spend as much time as possible with your family and loved ones, do things you enjoy doing together, and have at least one family home evening each week where you can spend quality time together.

• Listen to a motivational CD or repeat positive affirmations to yourself to restore a positive attitude, especially when you feel down and negative emotions start to creep in.

• Take time each day to do something you love that doesn't require you to make decisions or choices, something that makes you completely relaxed.

• Do something unusual, completely different, unconventional, or try new hobbies or sports you never dreamed of.

• Exercise completely free of charge, such as walking in the fresh air, going to the gym, or participating in activities such as yoga.

• Set goals to keep you moving forward, and reward yourself with small rewards when you reach your goals

• Learn techniques to quickly turn your attention and focus on the task at hand.

• Use affirmations throughout the day to instil confidence and positive thoughts and feelings.

• Always do your best in bad situations. Things may not be what we expect.

• Remember that this situation will not last forever. This is a temporary step and will improve.

The sky is your limit

The sky really is your limit and by following a few simple steps you can achieve anything in life. The key to success is to focus on getting what you want, focus on doing whatever it takes to get what you want, and change your approach to Stick to that new approach until you achieve what you want. Let's take a closer look at the steps.

Commitment

You should take positive action and decide exactly what it is you wish to achieve in life and set your goal, once you have set your mind on what you want you should go into it with utter conviction and commitment. When you are planning and setting out your goal you have to have firm conviction that you will achieve your goal whatever it takes, you should visualize your goal from beginning to end and see yourself achieving whatever it is you set out do.

Take whatever steps are needed

Once you have decided to go for it and have made the commitment then the next step is to start taking action towards reaching your goal, taking the first step is actually the hardest part because it means going out there and actually doing something. Thinking about what it is you have to do is the easy part as is saying you are committed to doing, but doing means facing the unknown and putting your plan into action and this stage is very often where most people fail, because fear stops us from moving forward.

Sticking with it

When you have made the commitment and taken the plunge into making your dream or goal a reality you have to have perseverance and be willing to change your approach until you finally reach your desired goal. Depending on what you're trying to do, it may take some time, but it's important to keep the project moving forward as it started. Keeping a journal from start to finish of your project will help you see how far you've come and help you focus on the results you're trying to achieve. Life is full of unexpected quirks and they all come to mind. That's why it's important to keep moving forward towards your goals through unexpected and difficult times. Fear is again the main problem and the main reason most people fail to achieve what they set out to do and give up. When you succumb to fear, big blocks just keep getting in your way until you are finally overwhelmed. The sky really is your limit if you try to reach it with patience and determination

How to develop your creative side

Everyone has a creative side, sometimes it's hidden and doesn't surface as quickly as others, but by digging deep and practicing to find your creative side and bring it to the surface, your creativity will grow. Here are some tips to help you get creative and expand your creativity.

• Make a List - Whenever you have a problem that requires creative thinking, make a list, list as many solution ideas as possible, and let your creativity run wild, greatly extending your creativity and you can make your site work.

• CHANGING LIFE - Getting stuck in a rut can sometimes cause creative block. Bring back the flow of your channel by making changes to your daily routine.

• Work on Bad Ideas - Even if you only come up with bad ideas, you are still creative. So if you work on a bad idea and say it's a bad idea anyway, develop it further.

• Work in Great Groups - Working in groups and brainstorming together is a great way to boost your creativity.

• Challenge yourself and others - When you challenge yourself by telling yourself you can't do it the way you normally do, you need to think of new ways around the problem.

• Scribble – If you don't have an idea for a solution, grab a pen and paper and use your imagination to scribble your ideas on paper. When you free your mind in this way, amazing things come to your mind.

• Encourages the Thinking Side of the Brain – The right side of the brain is where creativity begins. It stimulates the right side of the brain and activates and awakens the left side. Try exhaling a few times through the left nostril only.

• Hire a life coach – if you feel your creativity is truly depleted then consider hiring a life coach to help you find it, a life coach can help you to establish the areas where your creativity is lacking and work with you to strengthen it.

• Think like a child – let go of all your adult obligations, stresses, strains and worries and go back to your childhood, children have the best imaginations and their creativity knows no bounds, think like a child.

When you are stuck for creative ideas and they will soon flow freely once again.

• Relax – creativity can often become depleted if we are under great stress, learning a relaxation technique not only makes you feel better but can help to clear your mind, give you a fresh start and get your creative side flowing again.

• Use some mind games – keep a few mind games to hand such as logic puzzles, by taking your mind off your problem and solving a puzzle you are using your brain and using your brain leads to positive and creative thinking.

Creativity Tips and Resources

Everyone can benefit from creativity in their lives. Get creative with work projects, goal setting, home and family management, and more. Here are 10 tips to boost your creativity to help you with your home and work projects.

1. Stay healthy

Find an exercise routine that you enjoy and stick to. Change as needed, but keep doing some exercise. To sleep well. Diverse and healthy diet. Meditation, or enjoying something you do to relax, can help you focus your mind.

2. Discover new things

We do many things without thinking. These things become our daily lives - mundane and boring. Try something new. This could be like changing the way you work or taking a new course you've always wanted to learn.

3. Start thinking like Curious George

Ask yourself questions about everything you see, hear, and read. Why? As? What happened? Find answers to your questions. You can also keep an interesting diary and track all your results.

4. Read a new book

Choose something you wouldn't normally choose. Get it at the library. If you've always liked reading non-fiction, get a fiction book. There are many interesting books to read and a wide variety of genres to choose from. Your librarian will be happy to help you find new books.

5. Act like a child

Children are very carefree, honest and funny. Think about what you enjoyed doing as a child. You can paint, get some charcoal, get some finger paint, and go to the local amusement park, whatever a child does. Have fun!

6. Everyone needs a little time

Take time each day to just relax. If you want to meditate, you can use meditation. Don't make plans, don't pay bills... nothing. Do nothing for a while.

7. What if?

What was the end of the world tomorrow? What if you went to college for business? What if aliens were real? What if there is life after death? Create your own hypothetical questions and see where your brain goes.

8. Make no assumptions

Suppose something always annoys someone. You may think your boss is an idiot. What if he doesn't like his life and brings it up with his co-workers? You might think that the person who turned you down this morning was inconsiderate. What if you take your child to the hospital?

9. Write about you

Who are you? What kind of person are you Where have you been in your life When was the most important thing in your life? Why do you do things your way how do you live every day?

10. Talk to people

Listen carefully to what they have to say instead of waiting your turn. What must it be like to be that person? Imagine how they live and think.

Listen to your inner thoughts

We all have feelings about what goes on in our lives. They can make thoughts and feelings discouraging or positive. A simple example of listening to your inner thoughts is trying on a dress for a special evening. Put on a dress and look in the mirror and automatically think I'm amazing or shake your head and choose a different outfit. The easiest way.

But if you listen to it with an open mind, your inner thoughts can help you in many ways in your day-to-day life. Our inner thoughts help us to be successful in life, feel more confident, and live happier, more productive and fulfilling lives. You are the most valuable resource in life when it comes to making the right decisions and making the right choices. Just follow your intuition and it will automatically figure out if something is right or wrong and how to get the best results, and it rarely disappoints us.

Channelling your intuition is easy. Here's a quick way to start using your intuition.

• Start with the easiest way to develop your intuition and use it to make less important decisions. Examples include deciding what you want to have for dinner or which movie theatre or restaurant you want to go to.

• When it's quiet, it's easier to focus on yourself and your inner thoughts. So choose a room where you know you won't be disturbed when making important decisions and decisions. A good technique is to close your eyes and take a few deep breaths to fully focus on the question or task at hand and make sure it pops into your head quickly.

• Acknowledge that listening to your intuition can lead to mistakes. Your intuition is usually correct, but your inner thoughts can be misinterpreted and lead to errors. However, you should learn from your mistakes and develop and strengthen your inner guidance.

• As you accept your inner guidance, don't try too hard or influence your response in any way to confuse things. If you tend to go in one direction, you probably already have the answer.

Following the above is the easiest way to bring your inner guidance to the surface when you need it. The more you turn to it and use it, the easier it becomes. Just as the cartoon character "Jiminy Cricket" sang to her friend Pinocchio, "Always let your conscience guide you", the same is true in real life. Follow your heart, inner thoughts and feelings. When you lose faith and start doubting yourself, you become groundless and indecisive, go astray or get stuck.

Mental image works

One of the most powerful and inspiring tools we use on a daily basis is something that each of us has: our own imagination. You can use your own thoughts, insights, ideas and intuitions in your daily life to create change for the better in all aspects of your life. Some people have more vivid imaginations that come to life faster than others, but with a little practice we can form images in our minds that benefit us.

Use imagination as a tool

How you use your imagination in your daily life is up to you. Use your imagination to visualize anything and use it for almost any situation. Visualization works by making you see the outcome of a situation in a positive way and seeing that positive outcome in your mind as if it were actually happening, replacing the negative thoughts. It should be visualized from all angles and perspectives to make it as visual as possible. The mental image you build in your head should be as clear as possible how you want the situation to develop. Think of the imagination and imagery you create as blueprints for design and construction in the same way that architects use blueprints to design a project from start to finish.

Foundation

Start by building the foundation of your idea or what you want to change in your mind, and slowly build from the ground up by clearly visualizing every small angle of your idea. The foundation behind an idea is the basis for its success. As you lay your foundation, keep the following in mind:

- What exactly do you want to achieve or change?
- What are the differences?
- Can you achieve what you want by yourself?
- What would you need to change in your life to achieve this?
- What do I have to learn to accomplish this?

Once you have laid the foundations for whatever it is you wish to change in your life then you can go ahead and build up on your plan, visualize the project every step of the way as clearly as possible and seeing the project from start to finish build in your mind as accurately as possible. When you have the visualization completed in your mind then you can take steps to achieve what it is you desire, if you wish you can then note down the steps you took in your mind in writing to achieve the outcome, and follow these through from start to finish.

The key points

The key points to using mental imagery successfully for any aspect of your life are

- Focusing your imagination on one idea
- Forming as clear a mental picture or image of the idea and outcome in your mind
- Building up the idea from the foundations to completion
- Successfully executing your plan

Taking care of your mental health

In order to live a happier, healthier life you should take care of more than your physical health by way of dieting and exercising, you should also take care of your mental health. Only by having a complete system of healthy living can you be a healthy person, while exercise is important for your body it is also important for your mind.

Stress involves each person in a few shape or different with concerns approximately finances, task security, duties and relationships all taking their toll on our intellectual fitness. Stress is one in all the largest elements to disrupting our intellectual fitness and in the end our well-being, it's far as crucial to lessen strain on your life, as it's far to lessen your fat, sugar and calorie consumption to stay healthy.

There are many methods which we will cope with our intellectual fitness and remove a number of the strain from our day, a number of the stairs you may take to stay strain unfastened include

• Learn to manipulate your day and time higher through taking off sensible desires which you may manipulate to fulfil every day.

• Learn how to make use of sometime greater successfully at some stage in the day through focusing and finishing one undertaking at a time earlier than shifting directly to any other

• Remain bendy on your wondering in terms of finishing tasks, in case you can't accomplish them the manner you had deliberate then do it any other manner

• Take small breaks at some stage in the day, those will provide you with time to clean your head and get again on target and live cantered at the undertaking at hand

• Admit which you are best human and also you can't do the whole thing, admit while you want a touch assist and do not be afraid to invite for that assist ought to you want it'

• Learn whilst to say "no", at the same time as all of us love to do favours we will from time to time take an excessive amount of onto our plates and whilst this takes place we can't manipulate to in shape the whole thing in and strain units in

• Never try and over exert your frame, you may best accomplish that a lot in a day, through seeking to push yourself constantly past your limits will strain your frame and thoughts

• Learn to understand while you are beginning to get burdened and take instant movement to alleviate that strain

• Learn strategies which you may quick remove strain, there are an extensive variety of strategies which you may use, with a few operating higher than others and providing you with higher results. Techniques along with respiratory sporting events and visualization are very powerful degree which may be used to quick ease strain and assist you to refocus

• Positive affirmations allow you to address strain effectively, a tremendous thoughts with tremendous mind is a more fit thoughts and one to strain much less eagerly

• Always make time for quiet time, just relax and do what you love, and don't feel guilty about taking this time off.

Chapter 3: Overcome negative thoughts

Alleviate Fears for a More Positive Attitude

Fears and phobias can affect everyone to some degree, but most people are able to overcome their fears, and most fears and phobias are dislikes rather than actual phobias. Their daily life.

Although phobias and phobias clearly provoke negativity and constant negativity drags us down, some phobias and fears take root. There are many ways to get help, and the deeper the fear or phobia, the more professional help in the form of therapy or hypnotherapy can be recommended.

Understanding phobias

To overcome phobias and phobias, it is important to understand them. Phobias and phobias simply trigger unpleasant thoughts and feelings in certain situations. It can cause feelings such as nausea, vomiting, dizziness, a feeling of fear, tightness around the head, chest pain, shortness of breath, trembling...all of which we build up and take over in our minds and bodies. It's a feeling of letting go. Relieving fear means taking back control and putting things in perspective.

This is the basis for healing all forms of phobias and phobias. However, if you have suffered for many years, recovery will take time, but recovery is possible. Phobias and anxiety are basically excessive fears, and learning and relaxation methods can cure anxiety and phobias. It's a good start for you. There are many self-help books, DVDs, courses, and audio courses to help you get started. Any self-help material designed to deal with anxiety and stress can help, but there are many that are specifically aimed at people who suffer from anxiety and phobias.

Benefits of Overcoming Fear

The benefits of coping with and overcoming phobias and phobias are immeasurable, and those who recover and overcome their phobias and phobias see the world reborn with new meaning as their phobias are dispelled. A new positive attitude is born, leading to a happier and more fulfilling life, contentment with yourself and what you can accomplish in life, and ultimately freedom to do what your heart desires. .

Occasionally, even if you've been afraid for a while, when you're faced with a phobia or phobia, it's different than the intense fear that once held you back. Once you realize that the key to overcoming these feelings lies within you, the fears you feel will not affect you as much as they used to, and you will eventually abandon them completely.

Overcome dissociation

Dissociation causes problems with our emotions, bodily sensations, and how we feel about ourselves and the world around us. It is often associated with depression or anxiety or when a person has had a traumatic experience. People suffering from dissociation offerings have unrealistic feelings and are often afraid of going mad or suffering from a terminal illness. Things become almost impossible, and deep fears triggered by emotions can develop into social phobias.

Dissociation feelings vary from person to person depending on the circumstances that led to them, but common thoughts and feelings associated with dissociation include:

• The world around feels unreal

• Not belonging in the world

• A grey fog covering their vision

• Like having a veil over your head

• The world is moving at a faster pace than normal

• Confusion

• A terrible feeling of not being able to cope

• Unsure of yourself

• Others find happiness but not you

• Extreme anxiety

• Feelings that everyone is against you

• Feelings that everyone is talking about you

These are just some of the feelings caused by disassociation and these feelings eventually cause the sufferer to believe that they have to turn deeper inward to themselves in order to get back into reality. They continually watch themselves for any brief glimpse that reality as they knew it is returning, of course the more they turn inward and worry the worse the symptoms are.

Cognitive behavioural therapy can help those suffering to overcome feelings of dissociation particularly when the cause is severe trauma. Those suffering from dissociation due to anxiety and stress may be able to rid themselves of the feelings through self-help methods and the help and understanding of a doctor.

It is important to remember that the world hasn't actually changed, it is only your perception of the world and those around you that has really changed and these are only temporary thoughts and feelings you are having. Once you have conquered and overcome what is causing you feelings of dissociation, you will be able to see things as before. People who suffer from depression or anxiety-induced dissociation need to realize that the feeling is just an emotion and will fade over time. Instead of constantly studying them and wondering when they're going to leave, it's important to accept that they'll be here for a while and stop worrying. When you lose interest in your emotions and stop caring about them all the time, the world can return surprisingly quickly to the world you once knew. Because you can recover only when you lose the fear of the situation.

Overcoming Doubt

Overcoming doubt is easy, in case you do not doubt it, of course. However, maximum people entertain a detail of doubt in our minds approximately being a hit on every occasion we attempt something new. In fact, nearly every person is in a few manner plagued with doubt of a few kind. Take science, for example. Do you observed all of the medical development performed might had been feasible without thinking the triumphing assumptions on the beginning? Suppose you need to begin an enterprise or release a unique project. Are you truly certain that it's going to be successful? There is usually a touch worry or doubt on the beginning.

Despite your doubt, you can't permit it maintain you out of your final goal. The motive is simple. You should be organized to danger failure due to the fact its miles crucial for overcoming doubt. Dive proper in to anything it's miles without being making rash decisions. Don't worry, you may not dive in without the proper gear. You will examine all the feasible results of your scenario and you'll embody the outcome, anything it can be. This is the name of the game to conquering doubt. Have braveness to combat it out and you're certain to defeat it.

Belief is the enemy of doubt. Learn to assume definitely and accept as true with to your capacity to be a hit. Remember you may be successful in case you assume you may and you'll fail in case you assume that too. Your mind are self-gratifying prophecies so that you should forestall questioning negatively. Likewise, by no means pay heed to those who discourage you, who experience planting doubts in you and who're certainly wolves in sheep's clothing. Always be within side the agency of these humans whose mind and attitudes to existence in fashionable are positive.

When failure moves you possibly may not be lucky to by no means enjoy failure to your existence. However, you should apprehend that its miles a part of existence. These are the instances while failure fills your thoughts with doubt and its miles tough to muster the self-assurance you constructed up in advance within side the process. You cannot permit move of your commitment, irrespective of how shaken you're via way of means of failure. In fact, any setback ought to most effective set off you to double your solve to make every other strive at attaining your goal. In order for this to happen, teach your thoughts to construct your willpower.

Healthy suspicion

Remember that a certain amount of doubt always helps you gain wisdom and progress in life. But if it causes depression, lethargy, or seems like an insurmountable hurdle to achieving your goals, tap into your reserves of energy that can harden your mind. To live a fulfilling life, you must strengthen your will to succeed at any cost and weaken your doubts by any means necessary.

You can succeed out of doubt or in spite of doubt. Or you may have to accept the inevitable and compromise with the worst-case scenario that presents itself. If this happens, simply change course, regenerate the cylinder, and start over from the altered path. Defeat doubt before it conquers you.

Overcome a sense of helplessness

We all encounter some level of helplessness throughout our lives. For some, however, feelings of helplessness set in and begin to affect the way they think and live. Here are some tips to help you understand and overcome these feelings of helplessness.

• First, identify the problem, fear, problem or obstacle that makes you feel helpless and try to understand why you feel this way.

• Work on ways to encourage self-reliance, self-confidence, and acceptance of new beliefs that you can handle whatever the future holds.

• Learn how to deal with feelings of helplessness

• Practice conflict management and problem solving.

• If it recurs and you have doubts again, remember that this is normal and pick up where you left off.

• Always reward yourself for even the smallest successes

• Recognize that feelings of helplessness will take time to change. Always strive towards your goals.

• You don't have to aim for perfection all the time. Nobody is perfect. Everyone makes mistakes.

• Identify what you need to do to develop self-control, self-healing, and self-confidence skills

Feelings of helplessness can purpose us many issues in existence, the longer you sense helpless, the much less manipulate you've got over your personal existence; right here are a few not unusual place stories that arise via helplessness.

• You start to sense that regardless of what you do or how difficult you attempt you can't achieve existence

• You turn out to be over dependant on others round you that will help you conquer your issues

• You see yourself as absolutely incompetent

• You broaden a deep seated worry which you are not able to deal with a situation

• You turn out to be miserable, sad in existence and despair units in

• You consider yourself as a sufferer that continually wishes rescuing from situations

• You have a pessimistic outlook on existence in general

• You are afraid others see you as being frail and weak

• You turn out to be despondent due to the fact you run out of folks who are inclined to appearance when you with the aid of using fixing your issues

• You renounce yourself to the truth that you may continually be helpless, which you can't in all likelihood change

There are many approaches you could assist yourself conquer those feelings, the crucial aspect to do not forget is which you aren't by myself and you could take again manipulate over your existence and make crucial selections once more to effectively resolve your issues. All you want is to have confidence in yourself and dig deep and locate that religion and convey it to the surface. While all of us have the cap potential to conquer our issues ourselves, it would not harm to get recommendation from buddies and spouse and children so long as you are not counting on them absolutely to resolve your issues for you.

Overcoming internal conflict

Commitment makes it much easier to deal with life by making decisions, sticking to them no matter what, and staying committed without unwanted thoughts entering your mind. Inner conflict leads us to indecision and is an open invitation to stress and self-doubt.

We all have them at some point, but it's important to know how to deal with them, work them out, and move forward again with a positive attitude. You can focus more. Reduce stress, listen to your inner voice, guide yourself in decision making, take full control of your life, and achieve the life goals you set for yourself. Manage and achieve to lead a healthier life to a more relaxed and happy future.

Inner conflict destroys our emotions, leading to low self-esteem, low self-confidence, and depression. In that sense, it's important not to banish internal conflict when it arises and let it get out of hand. Inner conflict can develop in many ways, and can stem from indecision or deep-seated feelings stemming from unresolved problems in life, and can even stem from what happened in childhood. After all, you now are not dealing with unresolved issues, facing and dealing with them, building walls to hold them back, but instead of dealing with what has happened throughout your life. Here are the results. It is important to break down the wall, bring it to light, and start working on it now. Overcoming unresolved issues and inner conflicts is based on:

• Letting move of the beyond and ideals from the beyond inclusive of letting move of vintage conduct and emotions, coming across the proper internal you and taking note of the internal you

• Realize which you are able to assisting yourself and turning into the character you without a doubt are

• Learning to grow to be cantered and focused on yourself, figuring out what stresses you and why

• Making yourself permit move of the emotions and mind you harbour pertaining to from beyond troubles

• Visualizing the brand new you, the greater assured and decisive you till it turns into a reality

There are many courses, self-assist books, DVDS and audio CDS which let you to triumph over beyond unresolved troubles and so conquer and address internal conflicts. However there may be no magical therapy and it'll take time to remedy those troubles and begin seeing a higher manner of coping with and handling life. While a number of us alternate simply via way of means of the usage of self-assist techniques others get greater advantage from attending assembly businesses of seeing a therapist within side the early stages. It is crucial to realise but that you could alternate and best you could do it, whichever technique you pick out to take to get you there. It all essentially comes right all the way down to the equal thing, converting your emotions and mind.

Overcome intimidation

Intimidation can occur anywhere, in any profession, and at any age. Being threatened by someone is a form of bullying and can occur in a variety of situations, such as at school, at work by a colleague or boss, or when shopping.

Some people don't even realize they're being blackmailed, while others can get miserable day in and day out if they're being blackmailed on a regular basis. You may even be someone who intimidates others.

A person who is constantly threatened experiences many emotions, but there are many steps that can be taken to remove the threat. In order to be able to deal successfully with intimidation you first have to understand what intimidation really is, it can come in many disguises.

- Using force to get what you want from others
- Threatening to or using power and control to get others to do what you want
- Getting others to believe they are more powerful than you
- Using size or strength to get others to do what you want or threaten them
- Holding punishments over their head such as being fired, spanking or divorce

• Being quick tempered, angry or getting into a rage with someone to get them to do what you want

• Behaving in a manner that has others frightened to step up to you

• Using your wealth to get others to do what you want

• Using racial or sexual slurs towards others

There are many steps you can take to stop allowing others to intimidate you, the first step you should take is to look at yourself and determine if you're irrational, unhealthy way of thinking has allowed yourself to become intimidated by others. If you think this might have been the case then you should take steps towards

• Identify new healthier ways of thinking to help you overcome and respond to the intimidating factors

• Show your intimidator your new way of thinking and acting and showing that you no longer want to be intimidated.

• Develop ways to deal with people who react negatively to your new self

• See the consequences of new assertive actions

• Stick to your policy and accept whatever the consequences of your new behaviour are.

Once you've developed a strategy for dealing with an intimidating person, the next step is to find ways to build trust in your new self. The easiest way is to use daily affirmations or positive self-talk. Examples of positive self-talk include:

• I am a good person who deserves to be treated with respect

• I will not put myself in a superhuman position.

• I will take my life back from anyone who tries to blackmail me in the future.

• Don't be intimidated by others

• No one can intimidate me

Overcome the need to control

Some of us have difficulty maintaining control. The urge to control all aspects of life for the people around us can lead to many problems. So what do you need to keep in control or fix, and what are the ramifications? And how do you let go of the need to control yourself? You are struggling to control yourself if any of the following apply to you:

• You compulsively rush to help someone simply because you feel the job or situation should be handled that way, regardless of whether they ask you for help.

• Feeling needy in others becomes an automatic reaction to you.

• We firmly believe that things should be perfect or just right for people. Otherwise they cannot be happy in life.

• Feeling the need to change people because they cannot accept people for who they are

• I am a firm believer in knowing what is best for others, and I do my best to make them see things my way.

• You accept personal responsibility for the actions of others.

• You are compelled to advice or offer help to others.

• People see you as interfering in their lives.

• You have a strong desire to feel wanted and needed, which causes you to become overly involved in the affairs of others.

• I feel bad if I don't help others or solve problems.

• The most common adverse effects that such compulsive behaviour can have on a person include:

• You develop relationships in which people become overly dependent on you.

• You cannot remain emotionally indifferent when you come across someone who you think needs your help.

• You lose friends because you have to control their lives.

• You begin to neglect your own needs in favour of taking care of those around you.

• You feel guilty when someone's situation doesn't improve.

• You may get angry with them if they don't show enough appreciation for what you've done.

• Low self-esteem because you lose sight of yourself with others.

• There are methods that can be developed to overcome the need for control.

• I believe in the ability of others to solve my problems.

• Set boundaries between people who feel they need your help.

• Don't settle for needing approval from others.

• Accept that the only person you have control over is yourself.

• Tell people to stand up for you when they try to give you help or advice they don't need.

• Recognize your ability to change yourself when needed.

• Offer help only to those who specifically ask for it.

Overcome trauma

There are many thoughts and feelings associated with traumatic experiences. Trauma occurs when you are faced with a frightening situation, such as: B. Car accidents, fires, witnessing accidents, natural disasters, attacks on you, wars, etc. Many people recovering from a traumatic experience mentally block out the stressful experience, while others relive it over and over again. Trauma brings many emotions such as:

• Shock - Shock is a normal reaction to a traumatic experience, and the closer you get to the experience, the stronger the shock. Your brain has to process the horrifying images you see, and the feeling of shock sets in and takes time to digest.

• Disbelief - Many people who have experienced shocking situations firmly believe that what they see cannot be possible.

• Denial - Many deny that the event happened. They try to get it out of their heads.

• Emotional Distress – Even if you weren't hurt in the incident, you will feel the pain of those around you who were hurt.

• Anger – When you're shocked and angered, you wonder, 'Why did I do this?' and get angry at everyone.

• Blame – We often blame ourselves or others for what happened.

• Grief – Overcoming certain traumatic experiences can bring a sudden wave of grief.

• Depression - You may suddenly become depressed for a while after the experience.

• Fear - Fear often stems from fear and can persist for some time after the experience.

These are all the most common feelings and thoughts associated with traumatic experiences. These feelings can occur in no particular order or time. You need to understand that these emotions are natural and that your body and mind are how you deal with what has happened.

Emotions and thoughts fade over time. There are many ways to deal with them and help overcome them. Of course, the best path for you depends on the severity of your trauma. However, there are many coping skills that can be learned to overcome trauma.

- Taking about what happened and letting it all out
- Listening to and accepting advice from family, friends or counsellor
- Accepting what happened and continuing on with life
- Changing your environment
- Taking part in recreational activities
- Picking up your old daily routine
- Taking part in seminars

Chapter 4: Becoming an Optimistic Individual and Achieve Goals in Life

Developing your self-image

How you see yourself goes a long way to how you feel about yourself and how others see you and think of you. If you think positively on the inside then you will glow with confidence on the outside and come across this way to others. Feeling good about yourself is essential if you are to be happy in life and make the most out of life, it can make the difference of you being successful or failing, it is all about how you see your self-image.

People suffer from low self-esteem for many reasons and if they have been brought up feeling negatively about themselves then developing a positive self-image will be difficult, but not impossible. Developing a positive outlook is about changing your thoughts and feelings about yourself and if you have been thinking negative thoughts for a long time changing the habit will take time. But by adopting a new way of thinking and holding on to that new way of thinking, we can eventually banish unwanted negative emotions and automatically replace them with positive emotions in our daily lives. When this happens, your attitude changes, and your attitude changes where you might have previously thought that something was beyond your capabilities.

There are many methods which you could use to broaden an extra fantastic self-image and esteem, there are self-assist books committed to the subject, audio periods that you pay attention and follow, DVDS, hypnotherapy audio or attending counselling periods. They all but depend essentially at the equal principle, knowledge what self-belief actually is, gaining self-belief in yourself, ridding yourself of bad ideals and changing them with fantastic ones and studying techniques which will let you continue to be assured in any situation. The fundamentals in the back of growing an extra fantastic outlook and self-photo are

• Thinking approximately fantastic self-photo and self-belief and knowledge what it approach to you

• Getting to recognize yourself better, spotting your strengths and constructing on the ones strengths

• Moving ahead and continuously converting bad mind into extra fantastic ones

• Reflecting on what you've got learnt and seeing the fantastic adjustments you're making for your life

We all speak to ourselves at one time or another, and we can also additionally discover ourselves usually setting ourselves down and are very sluggish to reward ourselves.

This should be changed. We need to alternate unhelpful self-speak and update it with fantastic and inspiring self-speak, the very best manner to do that is by

• Getting rid of irrational mind and update them with rational ones

• Replace bad mind and emotions with fantastic

• Give your self-credit

• Repeat fantastic affirmations to yourself whilst wanted at some stage in the day

Change the Shape of Your Self-Image

While all of us apprehend the significance of ingesting healthful, exercise and dieting, only a few understand that converting our self-picture is simply as critical to main a healthful lifestyle. How you watched and experience approximately your self is going a protracted manner to bringing happiness and achievement into your existence and so that it will alternate your self-picture - simply as you deliver your frame a workout - you want to present your thoughts a work-out too. The first step you want to take is to decide what precisely its miles you would love to be and what you're already top at or experience doing. You may say you're top at sports, poetry and spending time with friends. The one factor you do not need to do is create a listing of factors which you do not like approximately yourself. This could handiest make you experience insufficient and preclude your cap potential to alternate yourself and your self-picture. By that specialize in the best in yourself, you'll be capable of speedy alternate your self-picture into something which you are proud of.

Visualization and affirmations permit you to understand simply how fantastic you already are. See yourself doing and turning into the entirety which you at the beginning wrote down. Repeat fantastic affirmations during the day to assist the brand new manner of wondering sink in and broaden your new fantastic outlook. By vividly imagining this new you, your thoughts will retrain till you apprehend that each one the belongings you visualize are true.

Consider maintaining a journal

During this manner you may advantage from maintaining a magazine approximately your transformation, you'll be capable of appearance returned on it and this may assist to reinforce your self-picture and toughen the brand new you. It is critical which you permit your beyond pass and suppose handiest approximately the destiny and the brand new you, you may broaden your new self-picture extra hastily via way of means of that specialize in what you're reaching and have not begun to achieve.

Goals get you there

Setting achievable goals and striving to achieve them will help you develop a positive self-image. Giving to yourself brings success in life. This is an integral part of reshaping your self-image. Set goals for work, personal, health, fitness or whatever area you want and work towards them. Set a realistic time to reach each goal and reward yourself when you do.

How you change your self-image is entirely up to you. There is no limit to what you can achieve if you put your heart into it and work hard to achieve your desired goals. If you stray from the path that leads you there, do not hesitate or get discouraged, get back on track and move forward with determination.

You promise to work hard to achieve what you want. Plan what you will do when you reach your ultimate goal. You should aim to make yourself something special, you deserve it. Keeping that in mind gives you the incentive to be worth it.

How Keeping a Diary Can Help You Succeed

Never underestimate the power of a journal. There are many ways a journal can help you be more successful in life. You can use it to help connect your feelings to your thoughts and your thoughts to your feelings. By asking yourself questions and writing down the answers to those questions, journaling helps you identify what motivates you in life and develop new skills. It helps you develop, learn new strategies for coping with life in general, write down ideas and plan, and learn more about who you are. A journal is an essential tool if you want to learn about yourself and be successful in life, and knowing about yourself is a must. Even if we think we know ourselves, we really do. Very few people. By keeping a journal, we begin to realize all the little things we do not truly know or understand about ourselves.

Develop your intuition

Your own intuition is your greatest asset and if more people developed an ear to listening to what we are actually saying inside then more of us would know the way to go and how to successfully achieve what it is we want out of life, simply by following our own inner guidance. Your own personal journal can be a great way of developing your intuition and listening to yourself and what lies within you, record all the little things that you might let pass you by, such as flashes of inspiration, premonitions or hunches about something, basically anything that your intuition is telling you.

Keeping a journal is essential because inspiration can strike at anytime, some of the greatest inventors and thinkers kept journals including one of the most prolific inventors in history, Thomas Edison. One of the most helpful things a journal does is give us the ability to look back on records and refer to them, for example if you encountered a problem and overcame it in the past and a similar problem crops up then you can reflect back and apply the same solution or adapt it for a more positive outcome. A journal can remind you of past achievements and this will last for a long time

Learn from the beyond approach which may be very famous and one that retaining a magazine permit you to accomplish is the "best-higher" approach, this approach may be implemented to any scenario that plants up in lifestyles and truly is predicated on you searching again at the scenario and locating what you favoured approximately it or what you skilled from it after which determining how you can do higher subsequent time or how you can have higher skilled from it. The key to improving from beyond errors and succeeding within side the destiny is to examine out of your errors however don't forget to cognizance for your sturdy factors in place of your vulnerable ones. If you pay attention greater for your vulnerable factors in place of your sturdy ones then very regularly this results in you unconsciously reinforcing them which then result in low shallowness and of route having a low shallowness is not high quality. It is most effective with the aid of using constructing for your strengths are you able to growth your shallowness and your shallowness is the important thing to know-how your weaknesses and correcting them and consequently constructing a high quality outlook on lifestyles which substantially will increase your probabilities of success. So with the aid of using noting down your reports for your magazine you're capable of appearance again on them and advantage a clearer know-how of yourself and the way you sense which in the long run determines how you believe you studied and the way you believe you studied determines how a hit you're in lifestyles.

Start early to combat low self-esteem

Health care providers know that there are many reasons why people suffer from low self-esteem, such as chemical imbalances, lack of self-confidence, opportunity, and discipline. However, the biggest cause of low self-esteem is, is the lack of positive feedback and affection shown to children at an early age.

All too often, children are born before their parents are mature enough to focus clearly on their own adulthood, family, and family values, competing with their partners for success while both are late. It means that you are trying to learn a good job by working until and we learn about life ethics and morals that are not under the influence of parents, and about these early family lives and the extended family. A lot at once.

Also, mature adults often repeat similar mistakes they made in their childhood before realizing they were following in their parents' footsteps. For example, many parents do not allow their children to keep trying and make mistakes on their own. And while many parents do not genuinely admire or admire their children, they often take their children and their efforts for granted in today's difficult, difficult and challenging world. .

Another important factor is that most of the time children genuinely believe that all adults are right and set their own values and feedback systems. Many of these adults who are living with the disease still struggle with illegal drug abuse, gambling, alcohol abuse, and other very important problems. I just haven't done it. Especially when young children are trying to follow in their footsteps. For example, what drug addicts and alcoholics overlook is that harmful physical, emotional, and often other abuses are passed on to children, while adults are forced to accept their own selfishness. It means that you are too obsessed.

In short, children and adults of all ages need positive feedback and people who genuinely show compassion and concern. Start young so that your partner and children make good, healthy and positive decisions. Encourage them, and when they fail at something, give them hope and encouragement to keep trying.

Also, encourage education regardless of your level. Too many adults "tell" their children that they want them to be successful, but throughout childhood refuse to comment on educational progress. So provide plenty of reading material at home, led by example, and encourage workshops, online courses, e-books, and more. Be sure to point out and guide your child or partner's strengths, such as subjects (chess, math, music, etc.), hobbies (handicrafts, musical instruments, singing, etc.), and service to others (volunteering, part-time work).

Grab it and show us your positive feedback. And reach out with human love, care and respect. You will win in return and increase your own self-esteem and love. Stop underestimating your worth.

It is important not to underestimate your worth. Because I think self-esteem is all about your thoughts and ideas about yourself. When you think about confidence, you look confident. This comes when people realize their worth and live more confidently and optimistically about the future. They are able to achieve their goals, gain experience, satisfaction, and happiness in life, develop effective and lasting relationships, and cope well with whatever life throws at them. People who recognize their worth are happy, capable of dealing with everything in life, and well-adjusted, capable of doing whatever they set their minds to.

Problems caused by under estimating your self-worth

Many problems can occur in your life simply by under estimating your own self-worth, a lack of self-worth affects your sense of well-being, causes problems with your feelings and needs, affects your ability to make good healthy choices in relationships, work and life in general and cause fears such as abandonment and problems such as people continually striving for perfection but never seeming to reach it. A lack of self-worth has been attributed to being indecisive, addictions such as smoking, drinking, drug abuse, compulsive shopping disorder and problems with eating such as bulimia and anorexia.

Realizing your self-worth

Each one of us is capable of realizing our self-worth, we do not have to do anything special in order to gain or deserve self-esteem. The key to realizing your self-worth is getting that little voice inside your head to stop putting you down all the time, it is our own thoughts and feelings that drive us to develop a low self-esteem. This little voice has developed over a long period of time, casting self-doubt onto ourselves until we genuinely believe that we aren't worthy or capable, it is our own minds that develop our feelings of low self-esteem, not some outside force. There are several ways to change your thought patterns and improve your self-esteem. This begins the process of discovering true self-esteem. The basics behind this fix are:

• Learn to recognize and stop self-critical thoughts

• Learn to replace your thoughts with more positive ones

• Get into the habit of correcting negative thoughts with positive thoughts.

There are many ways in which you can begin to set the pattern of changed thoughts but perhaps the easiest one is using affirmations, which are simple positive statements and using these to replace any negative thoughts, examples of positive affirmations could be:

• This is a new and exciting challenge – this could be used to replace thoughts such as this is too hard or I can't do this it's beyond me.

• I am a confident, worthy individual – replace this when you have thoughts such as can I do this or I could never do this.

• I can do anything my heat desires if I put my mind to it – this can be used to replace thoughts such as I'm not sure if I'm capable of completing this task or I don't know if I can complete what is asked of me.

All of these are simple affirmations that you can use to gradually change the way you think, which in time will change the way you feel about yourself and encourage you to realize your true self-worth.

Developing your full potential

While many of us are happy in life and do accomplish to some extent what we set out to do, there aren't many that actually push themselves that little bit further and go on to develop their full potential. We may be particularly good at doing certain things in life, but if we just have the courage to try and believe in ourselves, we can be better at it.

As children, we are full of great ideas that never stop because we believe in ourselves that we can achieve anything with an open mind. But as they grow up, the fear of doing the right thing, speaking up, or being ridiculed becomes prevalent, slowing the flow of imagination and ideas. We suppress our thoughts and this can prevent us from reaching our full potential.

There are many methods you may begin growing your ability, it is in no way too late. You need to bear in mind that there may be no proper and incorrect manner of questioning and regularly the purpose why others try and make you experience inferior while you voice reviews and thoughts is due to the fact they desire that they'd had the concept and braveness to talk up. So cognizance in your capabilities and capabilities and permit your mind run free, positioned them to apply and definitely excel in life.

In order to achieve success you need to recognize that you'll from time to time make errors, no person is ideal and errors are adequate imparting you renowned them and analyse from them. Characteristics that you may nurture and so one can result in growing your genuine and complete ability include:

• Working hard – setting your all into the whole lot you do while operating closer to what you need in life

• Having staying power – matters do not take place in a single day so have staying power and you'll be rewarded

• Determination – stick with your weapons and in no way supply in while matters do not pass your manner otherwise you encounter hurdles

• Commitment – be devoted closer to your desires and what you what to achieve, set desires in thoughts and do not permit something or every person stand on your manner of accomplishing them

• Organizational capabilities – the greater prepared you're the less complicated the street to achievement will be, plan out your thoughts to their fullest earlier than setting them into action

• Learn from your mistakes – You'll make mistakes along the way, but you'll learn valuable lessons and move on.

• Confidence - You need to be confident and believe in yourself and your thoughts. There can be no doubt.

• Be realistic – Don't set goals that you can't realistically achieve in a set amount of time. Always prepare for failure by setting unrealistic goals.

The two most important things to remember in order to reach your full potential are what you want in life and what you can realistically do to achieve it. Once you understand these facts, you can go all out to achieve what you want.

Boost your self-esteem with running

Running is a great way to boost your self-esteem, especially if you're a beginner. Running allows you to test and push your limits like never before. Every milestone you hit gives you confidence and the ability to take on the world.

Start slow and get big results

Even if you can't run to the mailbox without huff-puffing, you can still run and boost your self-esteem. When you run to the mailbox for the first time, whether it's down the street, around the block, or far away, you'll feel a great sense of pride and accomplishment. When you go out for the first time, you will probably walk more than run. But if you keep at it, you'll soon find yourself running more and more until one day you're running the full distance non-stop.

Don't overdo it and remember to start slowly. Your body needs to adapt to the new level of activity, especially if you previously led a sedentary lifestyle. Overdoing it and injuring yourself can be a big disappointment, especially after witnessing progress. Most people don't want to increase their weekly mileage by more than 10%. But do what works best for you. Some people can handle larger mileage increases, while others need to add mileage more slowly. 90% of running is mental

His 90% of running is just the mental ability to do it, regardless of how his muscles feel. Whatever your goals are, whether you can do it, finish a race, or run straight for 30 minutes, telling yourself to build that part of your brain is always a sure-fire way to build self-esteem. What happens is you have to come up with good things to say to yourself while you run. This is often called positive self-talk. Not only will this self-talk get you through your current run, but it will permeate you for the rest of your life, and you'll find yourself applying it to your work while washing the dishes or doing heavy chores.

Set goals

In running, you can set big and small goals. For starters, hitting a local 5K might be a good goal. They must definitely enjoy the sense of accomplishment. Not to mention something you can show off in the office.

Remember to set realistic goals for execution.

How to unlock hidden strengths

Have you ever realized that you have a storehouse of strength deep within you, just like everyone else? Most of us are aware of the fact that we have such hidden talents. Others know they have strengths, but they don't know how to draw on them and use them to improve their quality of life and live more fulfilling lives. Hmm. Let's explore ways and means to reveal our hidden strengths to enrich our lives. First, you must believe that you have inherent strengths.

Banish all negativity in your thoughts and actions. "I can't. Instead, remember that you have the power within you to face any situation and you can handle it well. Confidence is confidence, and gaining confidence is half the battle." Remember one thing. The next step is to explore yourself. Explore both genetic and acquired backgrounds. It's not that I've never done it before. Now you need to be more systematic. Write down what you inherited from your parents and grandparents.

If you think you inherited nothing, think about what they taught you. Is it possible that you have such strengths deep within you but do not realize that you can tap into them? List all the strengths and talents of your parents or grandparents. See if you can use some or all of these. For example, is music playing in your family? Have you ever noticed that your mother was very patient? She may carry it on her back without you even knowing. Have you ever found yourself naturally using words that other people you know don't know? Perhaps you are blessed with a strong physique, but do not know how to use your strength to your advantage. Explore, experiment, and finally use. This is a strategy for showing your strengths openly.

Educational strengths

Your acquired background seems easy to analyse. But we actually need to look more closely. Again, make a detailed list of strengths you learned in your training. What skills did you acquire? Are you making the most of your skills and talents? Have you considered the possibility of pursuing your interests, turning some of them into hobbies, and turning at least one of them into a side hustle? Use your inner strength to succeed in life.

This is not a one-time exercise. As your life continues to move forward, reviewing your strengths regularly will help you find unknown strengths that can help set you on the right path. Who knows, you might strike gold. I can't!

Although NLP comes in the context of influencing human behaviour through the adoption and application of certain established techniques and procedures, many newcomers to NLP may wonder what that is. I have. NLP actually stands for Neurolinguistics Programming,

"Neurology" refers to both mind and body, "linguistics" refers to the patterns or structures of language, and "programming" refers to coordinating the mind, body, and language to shape behaviour and achieve better results. Development of methods and means. In a way, NLP can help you in many ways just by learning about its techniques and how to use them to your advantage.

Change in perception

If you are interested in developing the personality traits and qualities that determine your verbal and non-verbal reactions to events in this world, you can turn to NLP. As a first step, understand that your perception of reality is subjective. Just as a map is only a microcosm of a territory, what you perceive as reality is not reality itself, but a colour representation of reality. No. Your reaction is not determined by reality, but by your perspective on that reality. NLP can help recognize this and reduce if not eliminate subjectivity completely. Then consider adopting a different perspective on reality so that you can change your reaction to it.

Why do different people react differently to particular events or situations? Isn't this due to differences in individual perceptions of the event or situation? What is traumatic for one person may be the same for another. Maybe not. For example, some people belittle or simply ignore verbal or physical abuse. Others may be affected enough to require psychological or medical treatment. The underlying philosophy of NLP is based on the premise that we can change our perceptions, beliefs and behaviours in ways that make traumatic experiences treatable. It can also make you immune to trauma.

Get rid of phobia

Similarly, NLP techniques can be used to remove phobias by first addressing the factors that cause them. You may be able to see things in the same way as the other person. You may be able to see the same thing from a whole new perspective. Or you can study people who excel in certain aspects of their lives, find out the characteristics or factors that contributed to their success, and try to achieve excellence by incorporating the same or similar factors or characteristics into your life. I can do it. By changing our belief portfolio, preconceived notions, speech patterns that represent our innermost emotions, and the subconscious that exposes our conscious reactions to the outside world, we can reduce our levels of unhappiness and increase our levels of happiness. . In short, as NLP practitioners claim, NLP transforms you into a new you, a happier, more effective you, and better able to deal with the world than before.

Organized for Success

When we are surrounded by clutter and chaos in our lives, this is a perfect breeding ground for negativity. Negativity is what creates feelings of low self-esteem and low self-esteem that hold us back in life and is the reason why we are not successful. That's what we choose.

Therefore, if you want to be successful and get the most out of your life, it's imperative to tidy up from time to time, remove all excess obstacles and possessions from your path, and keep your life open and free-flowing. Here are some simple points to keep in mind to keep your home and life clutter-free.

Replace old with new

This applies to anything you bring into your home, including clothing, utensils, furniture, and other items. If you're constantly buying new items to bring into your home, you can quickly become overwhelmed with items that are usually boxed up and placed in your basement.

Don't put unnecessary things

To keep your home clean, it's important to keep things out of the way. Items that fall into this category include junk his mail that goes into mailboxes, flyers, old newspapers, magazines, letters, or even car trash. Unwanted letters and junk mail can be quickly discarded, but car waste should be collected daily and disposed of immediately. You'd be surprised how much junk builds up in your house on a daily basis, just by keeping an eye out for stuff like this.

Throw away what you don't like

Don't fall in love with an item just because it was given to you as a gift. This may sound harsh, but it creates unnecessary confusion. Don't keep what you don't like, give it away to someone who does, or sell it. But don't stick to it.

Have a goal

For example, treat each room separately and say to yourself, "He wants to clear this room by 25%." When you start with a clear goal in mind, you'll feel more in control, organized, and accomplished. He has to divide the clutter into three piles: items that can be sold, items that are junk, and items that he wants to donate to charity. Start with a clear plan and goals in mind. This makes organizing your life a lot easier.

Don't hesitate

Be strict with yourself and don't feel guilty about throwing something away or giving it away. Once you start decluttering, stop thinking about it and change your mind about removing something from the pile and removing emotions. Stopping and thinking about each item in this way sows seeds of doubt and negativity that lead to confusion and a house full of items you don't need.

www.ingramcontent.com/pod-product-compliance
Lightning Source LLC
LaVergne TN
LVHW080557160826
845677LV00010B/1885
* 9 7 9 8 3 5 7 1 4 3 6 7 9 *